Copyright © 2017 by Nina Planck

All rights reserved

Published in the United States by
Small Farm Press
New York

ISBN-13:978-0692806067
ISBN-10:0692806067

NinaPlanck.com

The Egg Book
A Child's Guide to Chickens

By Nina Planck
Art by Nicole Stremlow-Monahan

There is no shape in the world
like that of an egg.

Eggshells come in white and a variety of soft colors such as blue, green, and brown. Some are speckled.

Big birds lay big eggs. Little birds lay little eggs.

Geese, ducks, and chickens lay most of the eggs we eat.

Collecting a warm egg is fun!

The delicate egg is protected by a hard shell. You crack the shell and hinge it open to get to the yolk and white.

The yolk from a chicken that forages outside will be a rich yellow.

The yolk is like a soft yellow ball. The egg white is like a pillow that protects the yolk.

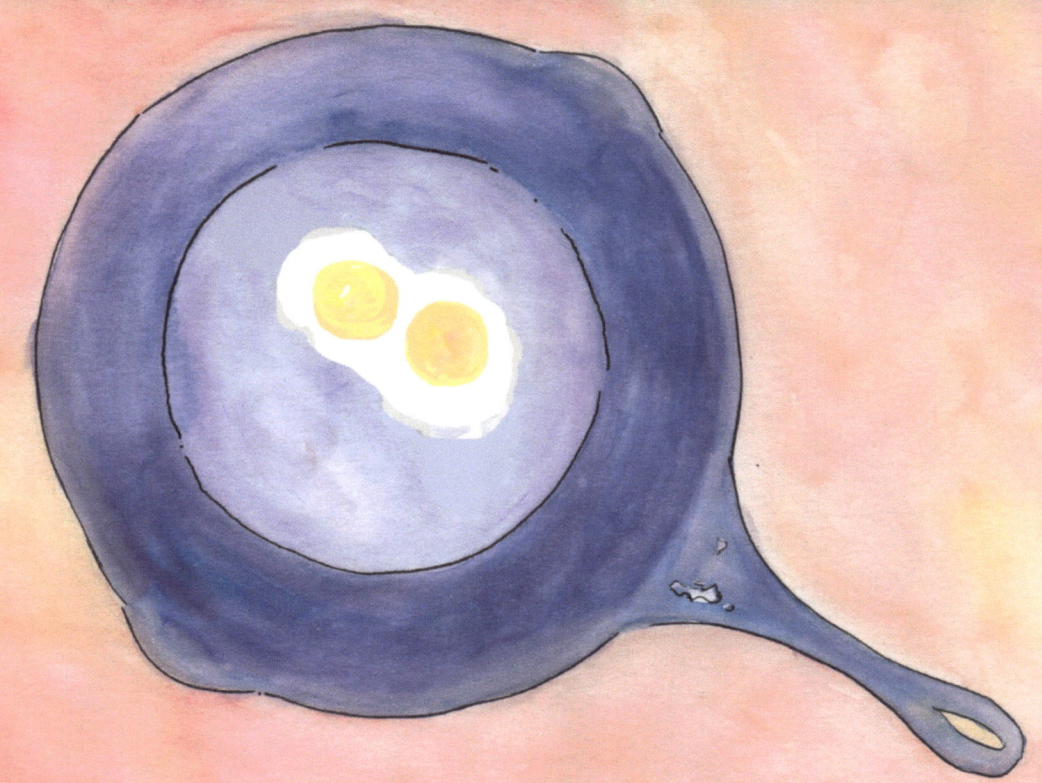

You can fry an egg. You can also boil one in the shell. Or you can crack it open and poach it in hot water.

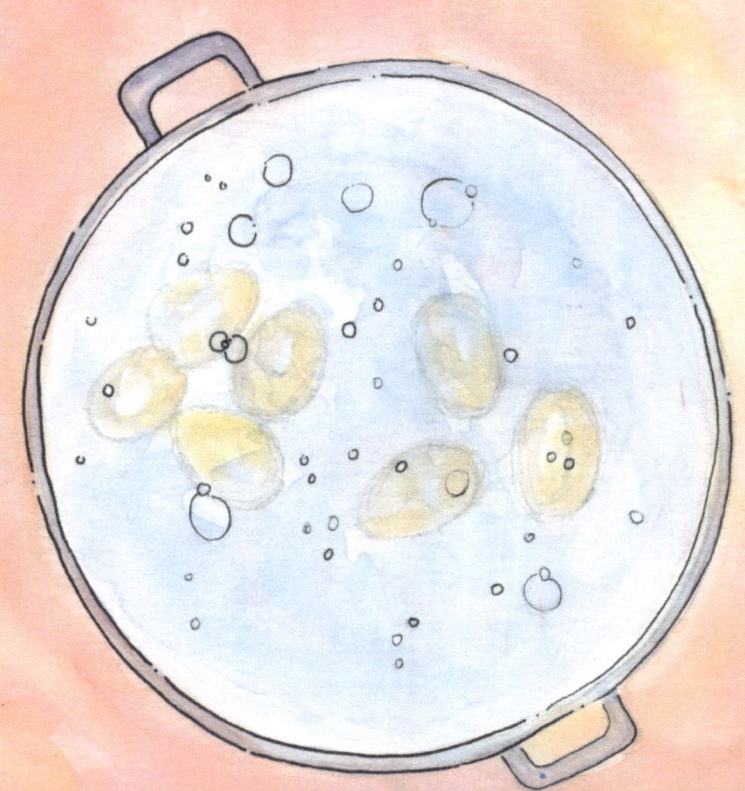

Eggs are tasty and good for you.

Scrambled eggs are delicious with smoked salmon and buttered toast.

Chickens and robins also love eggs...

... but they don't eat eggs like we do.

Instead, they sit on them. Their bodies and feathers warm the eggs.

In two or three weeks, something wonderful happens to the warm eggs.

Inside the chicken eggs are fluffy baby chicks!

Inside the bright blue eggs are scrawny baby robins with big eyes!

The chicks run around calling, "Peep, peep!"

The mother hen answers in her language, "Here I am, darlings."

The hungry robins open wide for food. They can eat one hundred times a day.

Chickens love to be outside, where they can scratch at the ground and feast on weeds, seeds, worms, and bugs.

When a hen is about five or six months old, she starts to lay eggs. A healthy hen will give you one egg almost every morning.

If you want baby chicks, get a rooster for your hens. A broody hen will keep her eggs warm until they hatch.

Before long, you'll have baby chicks.

Now you're a farmer.

Egg Are Tasty and Good for You

Eggs are one of the most perfect whole foods. One egg contains plenty of complete protein and all the healthy natural fats: saturated, monounsaturated, and polyunsaturated. Eggs contain choline (to build cell membranes and send brain signals); lutein and zeaxanthin (antioxidants critical for vision); vitamins B2 (for healthy skin, digestion, and many enzyme reactions); B12 (essential for blood production and a healthy nervous system); and selenium (used in enzyme reactions and multiple cell functions).

Eggs from pastured chickens contain more vitamins A and E, and more of the omega-3 fats EPA and DHA. These fats support brain health and healthy triglyceride levels. Eating eggs will raise blood levels of HDL, a beneficial lipoprotein.

When I was little, we kept summer chickens. In the fall, we sent our laying hens away to become soup, and we continued to eat our own eggs, laid in the late summer and fall, for much of the winter. Not very fresh, you think? But our eggs—even six, eight, or twelve weeks old—were still superior to supermarket eggs, partly because our chickens lived better than industrial layers.

Our eggs stayed fresh for another reason: eggs have a natural protective film, designed to keep the yolk fresh for the developing chick, a film we did not wash off. I still don't wash our own eggs, and I prefer to buy unwashed eggs from farmers, too, though in practice we eat them very quickly. Keep eggs in the fridge for three or four weeks or at (a coolish) room temperature for a couple of days. They will still be plenty fresh.

How old are supermarket eggs, anyway? The expiration date must be no more than thirty days from the date the eggs were packed. Most eggs are packed within one week of being laid. So the typical store-bought egg may be a month old on the day you bring it home.

Nina Planck

Recipes

Scrambled Eggs
Crack two eggs per person, whisk, and add one to two tablespoons of whole milk. Melt one tablespoon of butter in a pan. Pour the mixture into the pan. Stir continuously over low heat until the eggs become semi-firm. Optional: add grated Gruyère or cheddar. Serve immediately with salt and pepper.

Soft Boiled Eggs
Boil water. Gently ease the whole egg, shell and all, into the water. Let it simmer for three to four minutes. Take the egg out with a slotted spoon. While the egg cooks, make toast. Serve the egg in an egg cup, pointy-end down. Butter the toast and cut in long fingers. (The British call them "soldiers.") Serve with a spoon and a small butter knife (or egg topper) to crack open the shell and lift off the cap. Dip the soldiers into the soft yolk.

Fried Eggs
Start with one tablespoon of butter in a frying pan. **Sunny Side Up**: fry egg over low heat, but don't flip it. Cover the pan with a lid until the yolk is white and cloudy. **Over Easy**: crack one or two eggs into the pan. Flip the eggs when the whites are cooked through. **Fried Egg Sandwich**: make an over-easy egg over medium heat, flip it, and cook it longer on the second side. Put between two pieces of toast with ketchup. Serve all immediately with salt and pepper.

Poached Eggs
Boil water. Crack one egg into the water, easing the white and yolk out of the shell and into the water without separating or breaking it. Let it simmer for three to four minutes. (Or ease the raw egg into a silicon egg cup, and let the cup float while the egg cooks.) Serve at once over buttered toast, with salt and pepper.

Hard Boiled Eggs
Boil water in a large pan. One by one, gently ease one dozen eggs into the water. Turn the heat down so that the water simmers steadily. Boil for ten minutes. Remove the eggs with a slotted spoon and let cool.

Peter Wilkie's Easy Microwaved Eggs
A supervised child can make this. Crack one egg into a ramekin and mix well with a fork—don't skip this step or the yolk will explode! Add a pat of butter. Cook in a microwave for one minute. Add 30 seconds if it's not fully cooked. The ramekin will be hot, so be careful. Serve hot with salt and pepper.

Patrick Lango's Custard *(from The Real Food Cookbook)*
Call it a dessert or a snack, it's the sort of dish I permit freely. If you don't have eight 8-ounce ramekins, use a shallow 9-by-12-inch glass baking dish.

1 tsp whole coriander seeds (optional)
1 split vanilla bean, soaked in Armagnac (or 1 tsp vanilla extract)
1 qt (4 c) milk
1/4 to 1/3 c organic whole cane sugar (or maple sugar, maple syrup, or honey)
1 tsp chunky unrefined sea salt, such as Maldon or Jacobsen
8 eggs
1 nutmeg

1. Set the oven to 350°F.
2. In a dry pan, toast the coriander seeds gently and remove them from the pan. When they are cool, grind them into a rough powder with a mortar and pestle or the back of a spoon.
3. Scrape the vanilla seeds into the milk. Add the vanilla bean and ground coriander and heat gently. Let it cool a bit.
4. Stir in the sugar and salt.
5. Whisk the eggs until foamy, but not stiff. Add eggs to the milk and mix.
6. Grate a bit of nutmeg into each ramekin and pour the custard mix in slowly.
7. Set the ramekins in a pan of quite hot (not boiling) water.
8. Bake for 40 to 45 minutes or until the center is set and a knife slips out clean.

Deviled Eggs (from *The Real Food Cookbook*)
1 egg per person
1 T mayonnaise or crème fraîche (or both) per egg
1/2 tsp Dijon mustard per egg
splash of olive oil to taste
salt
sprinkle of paprika
pinch of cayenne (optional)

1. Boil water in a large pot. One by one, gently ease eggs in. Turn the heat down and simmer for ten minutes. Remove eggs with a slotted spoon and let cool.
2. Peel shells carefully.
3. Cut eggs in half and remove the yolk.
4. Mash the yolk with the mayonnaise or crème fraîche and the mustard. I like a little olive oil, too. Make it perfectly smooth. Salt to taste.
5. Fill the whites with the yolk mixture and sprinkle with paprika. Those who want the cayenne pepper know who they are.

About the Author

"A cross between Alice Waters and Martha Stewart," (*Washington Post*), Nina Planck is the author of the acclaimed *Real Food: What to Eat and Why*. Her vigorous defense of traditional foods liberated eaters who'd had enough of low-fat and imitation foods.

In *Real Food for Mother and Baby*, Nina takes up traditional diets for mother, father, and child. She dismantles common misconceptions and fears about prenatal and weaning foods in her typically direct style.

Nina's cookbooks, the ebook *Farmers' Market Cookbook*, and the gorgeous hardcover *Real Food Cookbook*, offer delicious and simple recipes using real food. Nina lives in Greenwich Village and Stockton, New Jersey, with her husband, Rob Kaufelt, owner of Murray's Cheese, and their three children: Julian, Jacob, and Rose.

Her other books for children are *The Numbers You Know: A Natural Counting Book* and *Bye Bye Baba: A Weaning Tale*.

NinaPlanck.com

About the Artist

Nicole Stremlow-Monahan has worked as an architect and art director. She illustrates children's books from her dreamy creekside studio in Washington State, where she also teaches art. When not working, Nicole plays with her children and pets, who give her good material for characters. Her chicken Goldie was model and muse for this book.

MonahanStudio.com

www.ingramcontent.com/pod-product-compliance
Lightning Source LLC
Chambersburg PA
CBHW041227040426
42444CB00002B/76